REVENGE: AFTER THE LEVOYAH

BY NICK CASSENBAUM

REVENGE: After the Levoyah was first performed at Summerhall during the 2024 Edinburgh Festival Fringe. It opened at The Yard Theatre, London, on 9 January 2025.

REVENGE: AFTER THE LEVOYAH

Performer	**Gemma Barnett**
Performer	**Dylan Corbett-Bader**
Director and Dramaturg	**Emma Jude Harris**
Producer	**Becky Plotnek**
Set and Costume Design	**Alys Whitehead**
Sound Design	**Adam Lenson**
Music Supervisor	**Josh Middleton**
Technical Stage Manager and Associate Lighting Designer	**Graham Self**
Fight Director	**Robin Hellier**

With huge thanks and appreciation to the individuals and organisations who have made this show possible:
Uncle Dennis, Shoresh Charitable Trust, Daniel Brodie, Tsit Tsit Fringe, Isobel Coutinho, Ira Coutinho Cassenbaum, Mandy and Phil Cassen, Storytelling PR, Soho Theatre, the Royal Court Theatre, Battersea Arts Centre, JW3, Emanate Productions, Mary Osborn, Gill Greer, David Feldman, David Schneider.

Gemma Barnett | Performer

Gemma is an award-winning actor, writer and poet.

In 2020 Gemma won the Off-West End Award for Best Actor in a play for her solo performance as Rory in *A Hundred Words for Snow* (Trafalgar Studios). Recent theatre credits include *Dr Korczak's Example* (Leeds Playhouse); *The Beach House* (Park Theatre) and *The Invincibles* (Queens Theatre).

Her debut short film *Bridge* was funded by the BBC after she was selected for the Talent Development Scheme and has gone on to screen at BIFA and BAFTA qualifying festivals globally. *Bridge* has won Best Actress and Best Short Film at multiple festivals alongside many other nominations.

Other TV and film credits include: *Casualty*, *Preggo* and *Please Carry On*.

Published work can be found in *Propel Literary Magazine*, *AUB Poetry Prize Anthology*, *Verve Poetry Press*, *Propel Anthology*, *Anthropocene Journal* and *The Passionfruit Review*.

Dylan Corbett-Bader | Performer

Dylan Corbett-Bader is a RADA 2021 Graduate.

His Film and TV Credits include: Sky series The *Tattooist of Auschwitz*, Hulu series *We Were the Lucky Ones*, Disney Plus *Star Wars* series *Andor*, *Tracey Ullman's Show* for HBO/BBC and *A Haunting in Venice* for 20th Century Studios.

Dylan has recently returned from New York where he starred in Kenneth Branagh's *King Lear* in the role of Edmund (which ran from Oct–Dec 2024).

Nick Cassenbaum | Writer

Nick is a theatremaker, performer and writer. Cutting his teeth in street theatre, he soon moved indoors, following his MA in writing for performance at Goldsmiths' College. Since then, he has written and performed two solo shows, *Bubble Schmeisis*, which has toured extensively around the UK and internationally and *My Kind of Michael*, which has also toured the UK. Nick has written two pantomimes for JW3, *Red Riding Hood and Big Bad Pig* and *Goldie Frocks and the Bear Mitzvah*. Nick is also a community theatremaker and has worked with his company Take Stock Exchange and independently with communities and theatre venues across the UK such as the Yard, Battersea Arts Centre, the Royal Court theatre and Soho theatre.

Emma Jude Harris | Director and Dramaturg

Emma Jude Harris (she/her) is a Jewish American dramaturg and director. She trained at Royal Central School of Speech and Drama on MFA Advanced Theatre Practice.

Credits as director/dramaturg include: *REVENGE: After the Levoyah* (The Yard Theatre, Summerhall and Soho Theatre); *How I Learned to Swim* (Roundabout, Brixton House and Bristol Old Vic Theatre); *Cabildo* (Wilton's Music Hall and Arcola Theatre); *Antisemitism: a (((musical))))* (Camden People's Theatre); *sorry did I wake you* (Tristan Bates); *The Agency* (Tête à Tête). Credits as director include: *The Retreat* (Finborough Theatre); *Ares* (VAULT Festival). Emma directs and teaches at drama schools including RCSSD, RADA, Oxford School of Drama, and East 15.

Dramaturgy includes *Watch on the Rhine* (Donmar Warehouse) and *Wahnfried* (Longborough Festival Opera), as well as research consulting on *Venice Preserved* (RSC), *The Mosinee Project* (Underbelly), and *Absolute Hell* (National Theatre).

Becky Plotnek | Producer

Becky (they/she) is a queer, Jewish creative producer, and founder of Plotnek Productions. Their practice supports nurtured delivery of projects, through individualised artist development. They platform powerful storytelling and experimental performance that is irreverent, joyful and often resistant to the status quo. Current artistic collaborators include Hannah Maxwell, and Nick Cassenbaum. They have also produced two Offie-award nominated Chanukah pantomimes presented at JW3, the most recent being *Goldie Frocks and the Bear Mitzvah*.

They have previously produced for artists across the UK and Europe, including at Barbican Centre, BUZZCUT Festival, STHLMDANS, Summerhall (Edinburgh Fringe Festival) and Battersea Arts Centre.

Alys Whitehead | Set and Costume Design

Alys is a scenographer and production designer. She trained at Central Saint Martins School of Art and Design.

Alys creates work for live performance and is interested in making work that is political, devised, experimental and innovative; with a particular aim to be as waste-free as possible. She likes working in close collaboration across the creative team to interrogate how design can be embedded in the dramaturgy of a performance.

Recent credits include: *Tender* (Bush Theatre); *Bedroom Farce* (Queen's Theatre Hornchurch); *This Might Not Be It* (Bush Theatre); *The Angry Brigade* (LAMDA); *Sorry We Didn't Die At Sea* (Park Theatre).

Amy Daniels | Lighting Designer

Amy (she/her) is a London-based freelance lighting designer, with occasional stints as a technical stage manager. A lover of theatre since she can remember, she studied English Literature at the University of Sussex, then fell in love with all things production during a year abroad at Stony Brook University in New York. She was the technical manager at Camden People's Theatre from August 2018 until September 2022, during which time she focused her practice from technical management towards production lighting and lighting design. She works on a wide range of performance, with an emphasis on the political, the playful and the pondering.

Adam Lenson | Sound Designer

Adam Lenson is a theatremaker and creative technologist. He has worked as a director, sound designer, video designer, writer, videographer and livestream producer. He is co-founder of the creative technology company Theatrical Solutions, and Artistic Director of Timelapse.

Sound Design includes: *The Retreat* (Finborough Theatre); *Reel Life* (Folio Theatre, Ustinov Theatre, Other Palace); *Gulliver*, *Casting the Runes* (National Tour, Pleasance); *Stills* (JW3); *Anything That We Wanted To Be* (Camden People's Theatre, Summerhall).

Directing includes: *Cable Street*, *The Fabulist Fox Sister*, *The Rink*, *Superhero*, *Wasted* (Southwark Playhouse); *Public Domain* (Vaudeville Theatre); *Little Women* (Dugdale Arts Centre); *Vanara* (Hackney Empire); *The Sorrows of Satan* (Tristan Bates); *Songs for a New World* (St James Theatre); *Dark Tourism* (Park Theatre); *Disgraced* (English Theatre Frankfurt).

Josh Middleton | Music Supervisor

Josh Middleton is a multi-instrumentalist, Composer and Musical Director specialising in Klezmer. He has worked with Klezmer ensembles She'koyokh and The London Klezmer Quartet, taught at Klezfest UK alongside Klezmer Scholars Alan Bern and Joel Rubin and performed with Frank London (The Klezmatics) and Merlin Shepherd.

He has toured extensively as Musical Director and accordionist with String Theatre (Tunisia, Turkey, Russia, Hungary, Serbia), Nick Cassenbaum's Bubble Shmeisis (UK, USA, Malta) and his ensemble Don Kipper (to much critical acclaim: ★★★★ The Guardian, ★★★★ The Evening Standard).

Theatre credits include *Indecent* (The Menier Chocolate Factory 2020, 2021).

Musical Director credits include *Watch on the Rhine* (The Donmar Warehouse 2022); *Red Riding Hood and the Big Bad Pig* (2023) *Goldie Frocks and the Bear Mitzvah* (2024).

Graham Self | Technical Stage Manager and Associate Lighting Designer

Graham Self is a theatre maker from Adelaide, South Australia. After graduating from the Adelaide Centre for the Arts, he wrote and performed with the award-winning sketch group The Golden Phung producing five Adelaide Fringe shows, a season at the Melbourne International Comedy Festival and a web-series.

He joined the London Neo-Futurists AKA Degenerate Fox in 2017 and has been creating new work with them ever since, including through COVID-19 lockdowns with the highly successful online show *Dirty 30 II: Electric Pay-Per-View*. He was Co-Artistic Director of the London Neos from 2019 until 2023 when he oversaw a transition to a non-hierarchical leadership model.

Graham has worked as an actor, director, technician, lighting designer, producer, stage manager, MC, programmer, administrator and front of house manager

Robin Hellier | Fight Director

Robin is a Fight and Intimacy Director, a certified teacher with the British Academy of Dramatic Combat, and he teaches at East 15 Acting School and Metfilm School London.

Theatre credits include: *A Streetcar Named Desire* and *Group Portrait in a Summer Landscape* (Pitlochry Festival Theatre and Royal Lyceum Theatre Edinburgh); *The Trojan Women* and *Haemosporidian* (Lyric Hammersmith Theatre); *Sunshine on Leith*, *Peter Pan & Wendy* and *Noises Off* (Pitlochry Festival Theatre); *Dear Annie, I Hate You* (Wild Geese Productions); *The Merry Wives of Wishaw* and *Henry IV* (Bard in the Botanics); *Tosca* (Opera Bohemia); *Faust* and Verdi's *Macbeth* (Paisley Opera).

'The Yard Theatre is a mecca for some of the most interesting theatre in Britain' *British Vogue*

The Yard reimagines theatre. Our programme crosses genres and breaks boundaries, because the artists we work with want to say something new, in new ways. We work with artists who reflect the diversity of East London, who tell new stories. They invite us into journeys of escape, euphoria, possibility and hope. Through this, The Yard reimagines the world.

We've developed artists like Michaela Coel, Alexander Zeldin, Marikiscrycrycry and Dipo Baruwa-Etti, Yard Young Artists like Lamesha Ruddock and nightlife collectives like INFERNO and Pxssy Palace. They've all used their vision and energy to give us new stories and narratives for what the world could be.

Recent work includes: ★★★★ *Multiple Casualty Incident* written by Sami Ibrahim, directed by Jaz Woodcock-Stewart, ★★★★★ *Samuel Takes A Break*, written by Rhianna Ilube, directed by Anthony Simpson-Pike, ★★★★★ *The Flea* written by James Fritz, directed by Jay Miller (2023 & 2024), ★★★★★ *An unfinished man* written by Dipo Baruwa-Etti, directed by Taio Lawson (2022), *The Cherry Orchard*, reimagined by Vinay Patel, directed by James Macdonald (2022), ★★★★★ *The Crucible* written by Arthur Miller, directed by Jay Miller (2019), ★★★★★ *Dirty Crusty* written by Clare Barron, directed by Jay Miller (2019), ★★★★ *Armadillo* written by Sarah Kosar, directed by Sara Joyce (2020), ★★★★ *A New and Better You* by Joe Harbot, directed by Cheryl Gallacher (2018) and ★★★★★ *Buggy Baby* by Josh Azouz, directed by Ned Bennett (2018).

theyardtheatre.co.uk

REVENGE:
After the Levoyah

Nick Cassenbaum

For my two eyes – Isobel and Ira

Introduction

With *REVENGE: After the Levoyah*, Nick Cassenbaum has written a play that is not just unapologetically Anglo-Jewish but joyously so, a play which revels in the specific nuances of the diasporic British Jewish experience, fish balls and all. Historically, the few British Jewish playwrights who have been permitted to enter 'the canon' have either downplayed their Jewishness intentionally in hopes of assimilation or commercial success, or had it erased by the gentile gaze of UK audiences and critics (Harold Pinter and Tom Stoppard come to mind). The novelist Cynthia Ozick wrote, 'If we blow into the narrow end of the shofar, we will be heard far. But if we choose to be Mankind rather than Jewish and blow into the wider part, we will not be heard at all.' Nick and I began developing *REVENGE: After the Levoyah* in 2022, with the wonderful actors Gemma Barnett and Dylan Corbett-Bader (who premiered the roles at Summerhall and are transferring to the Yard). Throughout the process of dramaturging and directing *REVENGE: After the Levoyah*, I have had a delightful time empowering our cast and creative team to blow into the narrow end of the shofar.

REVENGE: After the Levoyah uses a stacked dramaturgy, by employing both the archetypes of Yiddish folklore–including not limited to the *goneff* (conman), the *nebbish* (hapless, submissive man), the *erlicher* (sincere religious type), the *drayer* (manipulator with criminal intent), and the *boke* (dimwitted muscle)–in addition to the more widely recognised tropes of the 'heist' genre: the mastermind, the backer, the inside man, the mole, the driver, the muscle, etc. These two sets of archetypes collide and illuminate each other with delicious effect in *REVENGE: After the Levoyah*. While not every audience member will understand every reference, we hope that the combination of heist and *heimishe* will allow everyone to access *Levoyah*'s fundamental question: what happens when a community is pushed to breaking point?

Even as I acknowledge the need for more Anglo-Jewish characters, plays and stories, I feel strongly that respectability politics are not the answer to the representation woes of any marginalised group. Therefore, *REVENGE: After the Levoyah* is a love letter to Jewish Essex, as well as the Jewish East End, that depicts three generations of imperfect, complex British Jews grappling with personal and political grief, collective hysteria, radicalisation, and intergenerational wounds. When Yiddish play *God of Vengeance* premiered on Broadway in 1923, a moral crusade erupted, leading to the arrests of the entire company and an obscenity trial, and forcing playwright Sholom Asch to pen an open letter defending his decision to write flawed Jewish characters. Asch concluded: 'Jews do not need to clear themselves before any one. They are as good and as bad as any race. I see no reason why a Jewish writer should not bring out the bad or good traits. I think that the apologetic writer [...] does them more harm than good in the eyes of the Gentiles.' In polarising times, it's more important than ever to show that Jews are not a monolith. *REVENGE: After the Levoyah* forces the audience (and, via its extensive multi-roling, its cast!) to hold space for conflicting ideologies and beliefs all at once. There is a saying: 'two Jews, three opinions.' We have pushed that saying a bit farther (two Jews, twenty-four opinions, not to mention the opinions of nine gentiles, including a possible neo-Nazi plumber). So enjoy the disagreement and find truth in the space between.

Emma Jude Harris,
director and dramaturg

Characters

DAN, *twenty-seven years old. Lauren's twin*
LAUREN, *twenty-seven years old. Dan's twin*

The two actors playing Dan and Lauren multi-role and play all the parts. For annotation after the character names, there will be either (D) or (L) to illustrate which actor plays which characters.

Note on the text

Dashes (–) at the beginnings and ends of lines of dialogue are intended to indicate interruptions or the abrupt start or finish of a line.

This text went to press before the end of rehearsals and so may differ slightly from the play as performed.

'You Always Hurt the One You Love' by Des O'Connor plays. Gunfire, helicopters, and sirens join the song. The music stops abruptly.

LAUREN	Hello.
DAN	Er… sorry hi.
LAUREN	Tell them where we are.
DAN	Sorry, yeh.
	This is our nana and popa's house.
LAUREN	Sandra and Lenny.
DAN	We're in Barkingside. In Essex.
LAUREN	Er, it's in London.
DAN	Essex.
LAUREN	London. It's in a London borough.
DAN	It's Essex… and it's three in the morning. It's 2019.
LAUREN	There is a TV on a console table. The table is surrounded by wedding photos, some newer than others, you can tell by the brightness of the pictures and the size of the hairdos. The television is on a twenty-four-hour news channel.
DAN	David Baddiel doesn't like going to Chelsea Football Club any more. Says the Tottenham fans are ruining his Saturday afternoons as he is pushing the presales of his new book.
LAUREN	The beloved Maureen Lipman is ready to move to America, no Israel, no America. No… *Coronation Street*.

DAN	The ex-Chief Rabbi Jonathan Sacks is looking very serious and saying that these are the worst words ever said since Enoch Powell spoke about the rivers running with blood.
LAUREN	Labour Party member Chris Williamson says the party has been too apologetic about antisemitism.
DAN	Another Labour MP is talking about how the Nazis were Zionists and wanted the state to be formed. Eichmann went to have a look.
LAUREN	I guess his first visit was nicer than the second.
TV-NEWS 1 (D)	'Jeremy Corbyn apologised for all racism.'
TV-NEWS 2 (L)	'But not antisemitism.'
TORY (D)	'Jeremy Corbyn called Hamas his friends.'
TV-NEWS 2 (L)	'Jeremy Corbyn liked a tweet.'
GUEST (D)	'He did not see the problem with clearly antisemitic imagery.'
TV-NEWS 3 (L)	'Jeremy Corbyn spied for Russia.'
TV-NEWS 4 (D)	'Jeremy Corbyn hates Jews.'
	(*The TV voices begin to blur and overlap.*)
TV-NEWS 3 (L)	'Jeremy Corbyn hates Jews.'
TV-NEWS (D)	'Jeremy Corbyn hates Jews.'
TV-NEWS (L)	'Jeremy Corbyn hates Jews.'
TV-NEWS (D)	'Jeremy Corbyn.'
TV-NEWS (L)	'Jeremy Corbyn.'
TV-NEWS (D)	'Jeremy Corbyn.'
TV-NEWS (L)	'Jeremy Corbyn.'

DAN	A golf club is raised, it is shaking in the air. And it comes down…
LAUREN	SMASH!
DAN	It lands into the television, the screen blinks with a stock image of frummers davening at the Western Wall.
LAUREN	SMASH.
DAN	An Israeli flag.
LAUREN	SMASH.
DAN	A deli in Golders Green.
LAUREN	SMASH.
DAN	Angry protesters, people pointing.
LAUREN	SMASH…
DAN	A flickering image of Jeremy Corbyn…
LAUREN	SMASH…
DAN	Shatters.
LAUREN	But the golf club hits again and again and again. Until it doesn't any more.
DAN	I am at a party at a friend's house. Everyone is getting completely shika, dancing. Then as night turns into early morning the numbers dwindle. I am now one of the remaining core group. All of us dancing in the kitchen.
	There's a woman there, one who I have always had a bit of a thing for… you know…
	We make eye contact across the room… and I am a little bit excited. It is that time at a party when anything is possible.

	She dances up to me. And now my heart is racing a bit. We'd been speaking earlier… you never know how things pan out. She dances over to me… I smile… she smiles…
	Then she leans in and whispers in my ear…
PARTY GIRL (L)	'Dan…'
DAN	'Yes…'
PARTY GIRL (L)	'Dan…'
DAN	'Yes' I say…
PARTY GIRL (L)	'Can you tell me about all this antisemitism stuff in the Labour party?'
DAN	I look at her.
	I say… 'I'm gonna get a drink.'
	Not long after that I leave.
LAUREN	I am sat around a table. Surrounded by empty bottles of Scotch. The table is covered with green felt and has eight sides. Four of them are occupied. Jacob, Jake and Joshua.
	We are playing poker. And of course. I am winning.
	I say,
	'If we want to really change anything. Well of course we gotta have the workers taking over the means of production.'
	Jacob sneers as he checks his cards. His dad owns a clothing factory somewhere up north.
	He raises and says:

JACOB (D)	'Oh yeh, Lauren, and how on earth do you expect that to happen?'
LAUREN	Joshua sees the bet.
JOSHUA (D)	'Don't be so stupid, Lauren. Communism has never worked and never will.'
LAUREN	I went on a trip round Israel with these three when we were sixteen. Each one has made a marriage proposal since. We were shown the Golan Heights and schlapped up Masada. Being told that that was our land… we learnt poker.
	'Well, boys, the issue is if you continue to protect wealth rather than people it will only result in more poverty, death and ultimately, division.'
JOSHUA (D)	'God, we know who she sounds like.'
JACOB (D)	'Yeh, yeh, yeh and how are you going to change anything?'
LAUREN	'Sometimes you have to take matters into your own hands. Royal flush. I win again. Cough up, boys.'
JOSHUA (D)	'I hope you are going to donate all your winnings.'
LAUREN	'Course. Join a union.'
	I take my winnings home.
	See Dan's shoes in the hall and a trail of pickle juice leading to his room – heavy night for him I suppose.
	In the morning we get a call from Mum.
DAN	I don't pick up.
LAUREN	I do…

	'Your grandfather is dead.'
	I lay in bed. I cry.
DAN	Popa Lenny is dead.
	My name is Dan, by the way.
LAUREN	I'm Lauren…
DAN	My sister.
LAUREN	No you're my brother.
DAN	Twins, not identical.
LAUREN	Obviously.
DAN	Our grandfather is dead.
LAUREN	When a person dies you have got to get them into the ground as quick as possible. Then family, friends and acquaintances are called, texted and emailed.
	Here we are at Waltham Abbey, the grounds in Essex.
DAN	We are stood outside the hall where the funeral will take place. Everyone wearing black. Some ignoring one another. Talking about the dead, about Spurs, about getting back to work.
LAUREN	Women wearing strong perfume, fur coats and thick lipstick come and hug me. Tell me what a nice man he was.
DAN	Men in leather jackets, suit trousers and trainers shake my hand, kiss me on the cheek, ask me what I'm doing for work at the moment.
LAUREN	There are men in black bomber jackets and sunglasses mumbling into bluetooth headgear. Security.

	The rabbi calls Dad into the hall. We all enter a few minutes later.
DAN	Dad now has a torn shirt.
LAUREN	The coffin is in the middle of the room.
DAN	Rabbi up one end and men and women on separate sides of the box.
	The women are looking at the men.
LAUREN	The men are looking at the women.
	People trying to work out who other people are, trying to spot a crier. Some people miming over the coffin…
	'What do you want for lunch?'
DAN	I dodge my way through and stand next to my dad and his brother.
	The rabbi is a short round man in a black fedora. He shushes everyone.
RABBI (D)	'Ladies, ladies, please…'
LAUREN	It's clear the men are making more noise.
RABBI (D)	'Here we are at the funeral of Eliyahu ben Shmuel, Lenny Frieze.'
	The rabbi prays, sings, tells a couple of stories.
LAUREN	I stand next to my grandmother, she has an empty smile on her face as if to say,
	'I am sad… but at least I don't have to wipe that tuchus any more.'
BOTH	*Yitgadal v'yitkadash sh'mei raba… baagala uviz'man kariv, v'im'ru: Amen.*
LAUREN	My Hebrew has never been good.

DAN	Actually, it's Aramaic.
LAUREN	You know what I meant.
	The coffin is wheeled out to the plot. Lowered in, and people take it in turns to throw mud on the coffin and bury it.
DAN	We slowly walk to the car park. Through the rest of the cemetery.
LAUREN	People are cleaning graffiti off of gravestones with toothbrushes.
DAN	We are walking behind Uncle Laurence and Clive the Cabby.
CLIVE (L)	'It's disgusting. Happening all over again.'
UNCLE (D)	'How can they let it? There was a time when they would stick up for us. They were our party. Now look, they have this fascist at the head.'
CLIVE (L)	'Fucking antisemite.'
UNCLE (D)	'Hear what he did?'
CLIVE (L)	'Yeh.'
UNCLE (D)	'You?'
CLIVE (L)	'Yeh.'
UNCLE (D)	'Hanging out with terrorists.'
CLIVE (L)	'Can you imagine?'
DAN	As we get in the back of Dad's car we overhear,
VIV (L)	'Such a sweet man. But did you hear he smashed up his flat with a golf club the night he died?'
DAN	'What?'

	We get to our parents' house for a lunch of bridge rolls, chopped herring and chopped liver.
LAUREN	Depending on how much you liked the deceased you sit shiva from one to seven days. We are sitting for three nights.
DAN	Mum is checking for dirt on the bottom of people's shoes.
	Me and Lauren are stood by the table of food surveying what is on offer.
LAUREN	In walks a short man, with thin black hair combed backwards.
DAN	He wears a salmon shirt.
LAUREN	The top button open showing a gold chain.
MALCOLM (D)	'It's me, Malcolm Spivak. Heard of me? Course you have.'
LAUREN	An old friend of Popa. He grabs us. Kisses us.
MALCOLM (D)	'Wish you long life. You alright? The grandkids ay. Your popa loved you very much. Adored you. Went on about the pair of you all the time. Hope that gives you some comfort.'
DAN	'I guess.'
MALCOLM (D)	'Well I didn't say it for nothing.
	What fuckers we got here then anyway?
	Right. Schtupped her, beat the shit out of him once, owe him money, she owes me money…
	Know who he is? Fuck me, did you know what he did? Here, when it was all kicking off in the East End, yeh. All these fucking

	yoks used to come down and have a carve up… he… I am sure he won't mind… here, Alf… '
LAUREN	Alf is sat hunched in a chair, dribbling…
MALCOLM (D)	'Mind if I tell him what you did?'
LAUREN	Alf's daughter says, 'What?'
MALCOLM (D)	'Oh nothing. He got hold of some acid. God knows where he got it.
	Fuck knows actually… where'd you get it, Alf?
	That old fuck threw it in one of the bastard's faces.
	I tell you what, I have never seen anything like it. Mind you I was only twelve.'
LAUREN	Malcolm takes an egg and onion bridge roll and shoves it in his mouth.
MALCOLM (D)	'But it's always been kicking off.
	Listen. Me and your popa. We went way back.
	Let me tell you. In my life I have done some villainy. Lots of which I am proud of. A few things I have done that are crème de la crème. And your popa. He weren't adverse neither.
	There was the time we was doing the markets somewhere. Fuck… You know. Kent… out in the chum. The crossing?'
LAUREN	'You mean Dartford?'
MALCOLM (D)	'That's it. Yoksville. He always said you were smart. You been?'
LAUREN	'No.'

MALCOLM (D)	'See, smart.
	We was doing the meat me and your popa. I see these yoks. It's what you expect in Kent init. The head of them, tall, blond, face like a pig, turns to us and gives a big hoike and spits on the ground. "Kike" he says.
	I thought, fuck me. Kept my cool. Lenny gives me a kock.'
LAUREN	'A kock?'
DAN	'A kock?'
MALCOLM (D)	'You know, a look. What's wrong with you both? A look?'
LAUREN	'Oh... a look?'
MALCOLM (D)	'A look yeh. But not any look... the look. A look where we know what's gonna happen, and how it's gonna happen.
	We pop out the back of the van later to have a fag. Painted on the van was a big red swastika.
	Once again me and Lenny share that look. Longer this time.
	The thing is, if you are gonna fuck with butchers you gotta know that that's a stupid thing to do isn't it? Butchers come prepared. Now if we were florists I would be worried. You got your scissors but that's about it, there is only so much damage the thorns on a rose can do. What you gonna do, arrange them to death? No, we were doing butchery.
	We finished packing up. We always had a nice bit of offal left over. Lenny let me

	take as much of that home as I liked. I love liver so I was like a pig in shit.
	Then we thought you know what... how about a G and T? We looked for the yokiest pub we could find. Weren't hard. As I said... Dartford. We walked in, and lo and behold, there were the pink pig yok faces from earlier.
	Well we showed them what a couple of butchers could do.
	Understand?'
LAUREN	'Yeh.'
MALCOLM (D)	'It's in your blood. Right. I'm going to pay my respects.'
LAUREN	He walks over to the mourners. Shakes Dad's hand and kisses Nana.
DAN	I say to Lauren, 'What the fuck was that?'
LAUREN	'I don't know. But I liked it.'
DAN	Back to the table of food. I see the fish balls and stuff a couple in my mouth.
	Cousin Melvin stuffs a couple in each pocket and a bridge roll in the back one. Make eye contact, say nothing.
	The room falls into prayer again, but I don't go in.
LAUREN	I get summoned back to the kitchen.
	Aunty Eileen is sat at the kitchen table portioning off fish goujons into zip-lock bags.
EILEEN (D)	'Here, Lauren, when are you going to get married, have a baby?'

MUM (L)	'Don't ask her that.'
LAUREN	Mum says as she walks in holding a tray of plates. Each plate has half a beigel, a tiny bit of pickled herring and a boiled egg.
MUM (L)	'She'll get the hump.'
EILEEN (D)	'It's about time, Lauren.'
MUM (L)	'I don't know why she doesn't just marry that Joshua?'
LAUREN	'Mum.'
EILEEN (D)	'Denise's Joshua? So handsome.'
MUM (L)	'So handsome, and has always had an eye on you ,Lauren.
	It's beshert. I know it is.'
LAUREN	'Stop.'
EILEEN (D)	'Any herring put it aside my Nigel will eat it. He's like a seal.'
MUM (L)	'Smells like one too.'
EILEEN (D)	'You should know.'
LAUREN	As I try to sneak out of the kitchen to avoid any more baby chat, a cold hard arthritic hand lands on my shoulder. It's Eileen.
EILEEN (D)	'Here, sweetheart. You shouldn't cook in a time like this.'
LAUREN	She hands me a zip-lock bag of goujons.
	'Thanks.'
DAN	I am in the hallway. I see it. I see it in the corner, the golf club. It is dented on the long bit and scratched on the head. I hold

	the grip, feel where his fingers would have been gripping on. I smell the rubber…
MUM (L)	'What are you doing?'
DAN	'Nothing.'
MUM (L)	'You smelling the golf club?'
DAN	It's Mum.
	'Yes.'
MUM (L)	'Why?'
DAN	'Dunno.'
MUM (L)	'Aw, he used to love taking you to golf when you was a kid. Such a special bond you two had, eh?
	Well, you're not having it. You've got enough shit in your flat.'
DAN	In the morning I am woken by Mum calling me.
	I don't answer.
	I look at the phone, already four missed calls from her… She calls again.
	'Yes I took the golf club.'
LAUREN	I get a call.
	It's Malcolm.
MALCOLM (D)	'Let's have lunch. I'll text you the address.'
DAN	We go to Borehamwood.
LAUREN	Malcolm is sitting in a café waiting. He is reading *The Sun*. On the cover it says 'Jezza's Jihadi Comrades'. He sees us, waves us over.
	Before we have even sat down:

MALCOLM (D)	'Listen, the pair of you. I've got to tell you something. I am on the way out. I haven't got much time left. Soon I will be like your grandad. Brown bread. Six feet under. Like a dodo. Now I want to leave with a bang, do something good. You're young. You both look capable. I am told I can trust you yeh?'
LAUREN	'What are you talking about?'
MALCOLM (D)	'What am I talking about? Look around you. Look at this…'
DAN	He holds up the newspaper and points to a picture of Jeremy Corbyn.
LAUREN	'What about it?'
MALCOLM (D)	'What about it… this man… this man don't like us. Don't like us at all.
	He wants to lead this country… And I for one want to do something about it.
	Hold on. Let's get something to eat.
	Sweetheart… sweetheart.'
LAUREN	Dan and I look at each other.
DAN	'He's nuts…'
LAUREN	'Do something about it…'
DAN	I'm wondering what's the shortest amount of time we can spend without seeming rude.
	'I've eaten.' I say.
MALCOLM (D)	'Do me a favour. You'll have something else.'
LAUREN	The waitress comes over.

MALCOLM (D)	'Right, three bowls of chicken soup, we'll share a plate of tongue. Get him a chopped-liver sandwich. Drink? Three lemon teas.'
WAITRESS (L)	'We don't do soup.'
MALCOM (D)	'What do you mean you don't do soup.'
WAITRESS (L)	'We don't do soup.'
MALCOLM (D)	'Fucksake. You got a pot back there? Here's a tenner. Go down Tesco's buy a couple of stock cubes and a bag of lockshen. And hurry up. I feel like I'm getting a cold.'
LAUREN	She goes.
MALCOLM (D)	'Where was I? Oh yeh. Listen. I wasn't born yesterday yeh? I am an old man. I have seen things. Seen a lot of things. I was in a fucking pram during the battle of Cable Street. I know when things are about to go mechula.'
LAUREN	'Mechula? What's that?'
MALCOLM (D)	'Your grandad teach you nothing? Mechula. Tits up. End of the road. Game fucking over. Right. A time comes in every yid's life where they either sit around and do fuck all and wait for something awful to happen or they do something. Stand up and fucking do something.'
LAUREN	At this point he looks around the café. Makes sure no one is near. I lean in. I'm on the edge of my seat.

DAN	The waitress comes up to the table and throws down three bowls of yellow liquid.
MALCOLM (D)	'What no kneidlach?'
WAITRESS (L)	'Your tongue is coming.'
LAUREN	He waits until she is gone.
DAN	He takes a long slurp of the soup. Then says…
MALCOLM (D)	'We are going to get Jeremy Corbyn.'
LAUREN	'What do you mean "get"?'
MALCOLM (D)	'I mean get… grab… chup… kidnap. How much clearer?'
LAUREN	'Are you joking?'
MALCOLM (D)	'Do I look like I am joking? I'm too old to joke. I haven't told a joke in fifteen years. I have never been more serious.

He is the reason Jews are scared. Him. That's it. Him. He is the reason, yeh. Him. Shit.

And before this disease that is in my bones takes over and turns me into an emaciated mess I am doing something about it.

Dan, you drive yeh? You got a car. Your grandad always said you sit on your tuchus playing video games? Proud of you he was. Sharp senses it gives you.' |
| LAUREN | Fuck me. |
| DAN | 'Nissan Micra.' |
| MALCOLM (D) | 'Perfect. And you, Lauren. I got something special planned for you. You're special. I can feel it. I can tell…

You're just like Lenny. Got the same glint in your eye. |

	Your grandad died smashing up a TV. He had such potential. Don't you want to do better than that? Well? What do you say? You in?'
DAN	'No.'
LAUREN	'Dan.'
DAN	'Lauren.'
MALCOLM (D)	'Go home. Think about it. Sleep on it. But you know where I am. Things have got to change. Before there is no way back.
	Go home. Call me. Let's do something.'
DAN	We get home.
LAUREN	Next day. I decide to go and see Nana. Not nice being at home alone at a time like this. So I head over to Barkingside.
	I ring on the door of the flats and I wait for her to shuffle to the intercom to let me in.
NANA (D)	'Who is it?'
LAUREN	'Nana, it's me.'
NANA (D)	'Who?'
LAUREN	'Me, Nana, it's Lauren.'
NANA (D)	'Oh Lauren. Lovely. Come in.'
LAUREN	By the time I get to her door it is already open and she is sat in a reclining chair with her feet up. Wearing a pink fluffy dressing gown. A *Daily Mail* paper is strewn in front of her.
NANA (D)	'Where's your brother?'
LAUREN	'At home.'
NANA (D)	'God forbid he should visit too. Tea please.'

LAUREN	'Course, Nana.'
	Nana has all old photos set up in a semi-circle facing her on the coffee table.
NANA (D)	'Look how handsome your popa was. Wasn't he? Shame what age does to you.
	'Ere look that's him with that Malcolm on their stall. Good days.'
LAUREN	I look at the black-and-white photo of the two men holding up what I think is a pig's carcass and smiling.
	'Nana, what are you going to do now?'
NANA (D)	'I don't know. After you've gone I might have a nap.'
LAUREN	'No I mean from now on. Now he's gone.'
NANA (D)	'Lauren, give me a break. He's only been under the ground twenty-five minutes. I am not ready for a shidduch yet.
	Besides, times are different now. I am an old lady. I am on my own. It's dangerous out there. Seen all of this? Look. It's frightening out there.
	Your grandfather knew. He knew.'
LAUREN	'Is it?'
NANA (D)	'I feel sorry for you kids. Living through all of this.
	Genie's taken off her mezuzah you know.'
LAUREN	'Nana, how about we go out for lunch? Get some fish and chips?
	My treat.'
NANA (D)	'Save your money. I've got meals on wheels coming over in a bit.'

LAUREN	'Well why don't we just go for a little walk? Go have a mooch down the high street?'
NANA (D)	'Lauren. I am not going out.'
LAUREN	'Why not?' Bit of fresh air…'
NANA (D)	'I can't. It's dangerous. You've seen the news. No. Lauren. No. I can't. Please. Enough. I am not leaving this flat.'
LAUREN	'Nana, but… '
NANA (D)	'No. No. No. Please. I can't. I can't. Not with all of that out there.
	How about another tea? Yeh?'
DAN	I am on the sofa playing on my Switch and eating fish goujons out of a zip-lock bag.
	Lauren walks through the door.
LAUREN	'She won't leave the house.'
DAN	'Who?'
LAUREN	'Nana. Scared.'
DAN	'Shame.'
LAUREN	'Dan, she can't just live the rest of her days alone in that flat, cos she is too scared to go outside.'
DAN	Just then the doorbell rings.
LAUREN	'Who's that?
PLUMBER (D)	'Here to fix the boiler.'
LAUREN	The man in his blue overalls comes through into the kitchen.
	He pulls out his tools and begins work.
PLUMBER (D)	'Tea?'

LAUREN	'Okay… no milk though. Don't have it in.'
PLUMBER (D)	'Ah… vegan?'
LAUREN	'No, IBS.'
PLUMBER (D)	'I see you've got one of those things on your front door.
	One of those Jew boxes is it?'
LAUREN	Me and Dan share a look.
DAN	At this point, I leave the kitchen. Not today.
LAUREN	'You mean our Mezuzah.'
PLUMBER (D)	'Is that right?'
LAUREN	'Yeh.'
PLUMBER (D)	'You Jews?'
LAUREN	'Yes.' I put the kettle on.
PLUMBER (D)	'Interesting.'
LAUREN	I watch him fiddle around with his tools. This shaven-headed six-foot-something man on a ladder.
	'Is it,' I say.
PLUMBER (D)	'Yeh, I mean I do have some admiration for you Jews…
	You seem to own everything. Run everything.
	Quite a racket you got going on.'
LAUREN	He rolls up his sleeve. There is the end of a tattoo, black ink. Thick black lines.
	Could it be?
	No, it couldn't be.

PLUMBER (D)	'Yeh, yeh. And that's the thing isn't it. You never can tell.
	Like you could be English to look at. Know what I mean?'
LAUREN	'I suppose.' I say.
	It must be. It has to be.
	There is a Nazi in my kitchen. There is a Nazi fixing the boiler in my kitchen.
	Stay calm, Lauren. Stay calm. The noise of the kettle boiling gets louder and it clicks.
PLUMBER (D)	'Where's that tea?'
LAUREN	'Of course.'
	I turn to the kettle and pour the hot water into the mug.
	My hands are shaking. I turn with the tea in hand.
	'Sugar?'
	And as I turn, he has already got off his ladder and is stood right behind me. Like this close. So close I could kiss him. I can smell the Monster on his breath.
	His eyes are looking right into mine.
	I think 'This is it. This is the end.'
	He snatches the tea out of my hand. Takes a massive slurp.
PLUMBER (D)	'Ta.'
LAUREN	He gets back up the ladder.
PLUMBER (D)	'You know what I never understood? How you lot have got away with it for so long.'

LAUREN	As he is up his little ladder fiddling with screws, hammers, wrenches, I think to myself… 'What would Malcolm do… '
	I think… something.
	He'd do something. I go behind him. And I go up to the ladder.
	I give the ladder a little kick. More of a tap. You know what, barely touched it. Barely at all. Like it was a nothing.
	But fuck he must have been a bit wonky. Cos he shot down. Falls off the ladder. Mug in hand. And as his arms are waving in the air like a baby pigeon he shouts,
PLUMBER (D)	'Fucking Kike!'
LAUREN	And his head hits the kitchen counter. He's out cold.
	'Fuck. Fuck. Fuck.
	Dan… Dan… Dan…'
DAN	'What? What happened? What is it? I didn't eat the stupid goujons!'
LAUREN	'Dan, look.'
DAN	'Oh my god. What? What happened?'
LAUREN	'He was going to attack me. He's a Nazi. Look. Look at him.'
	We get closer to the tattoo… it's not a swastika… but a big black thick cross with a circle round it.
	'That's a Nazi thing right?'
DAN	'Fuck… I don't know. Fuck.'
LAUREN	Fuck…

DAN	'Hello… hello… hello…'
LAUREN	Nothing…
DAN	'Hello… this is what you meant by doing something?'
LAUREN	'I don't know. He's not waking up.'
DAN	'Should I call an ambulance?'
LAUREN	'Schmok. What good would that do. I'd go down.
	I know… call Malcolm.'
	Within in an hour he's here.
MALCOM (D)	'Don't worry. I'll sort this. You two sit down. Have a sandwich.'
LAUREN	With him is a squat elderly bald man that looks like a barrel with arms and legs.
MALCOLM (D)	'This is Moishy. A survivor from Belsen and has been on the run for donkey's for renting out his council flat and selling moody gear.'
MOISHY (L)	'Prada, Gucci – whatever you want?'
MALCOM (D)	'At ninety-four he's still the toughest fucking yid I know.'
MOISHY (L)	'You got me out of bed for this?'
MALCOLM (D)	'He still alive?'
LAUREN	Moishy grabs the man's head with his thick lappers and gives his neck a quick crack.
MOISHY (L)	'Not any more.'
LAUREN	'He was a Nazi. He was going to attack me.'
MALCOLM (D)	'I know, sweetheart. You did the right thing.'

DAN	'She did?'
MALCOLM (D)	'Absolutely.'
LAUREN	Moishy looks Dan up and down and says:
MOISHY (L)	'And where the fuck were you?'
DAN	'I... I... I...'
LAUREN	'He was busy.'
MALCOM (D)	'I knew I saw something in you, Lauren.
	Take down this address. Meet me there tomorrow morning. Ten a.m.
	And, Daniel. You better be there with her. And don't be late.'
LAUREN	'Okay. What's going on?'
MOISHY (L)	'Just do what he says.'
MALCOM (D)	'You'll see.'
LAUREN	They leave after forty-five minutes with the body. Kitchen spotless.
DAN	'Fuck.'
LAUREN	'What's wrong?'
DAN	'Fuck.'
LAUREN	'Oh shut up.'
	I am trying to hold it together but my heart feels like it is going to explode.
DAN	'Don't you tell me to shut up. You just killed a man.'
LAUREN	'"You?" You mean "we"?'
DAN	'No.'
LAUREN	'You didn't stop me, Daniel.'

DAN	'I was in my room. I was busy. I was playing on my Switch.
	Fuck. I can't… fuck.
	I am going to go for a walk. Clear my head.
	Fuck.'
LAUREN	'Hey, Dan… you better keep shtum. Yeh.'
	Dan grabs his coat and walks out.
	I slide with my back against the kitchen counter trying to catch my breath. What the fuck?
DAN	I walk. I walk and I walk and I walk. I don't know where I am going. I just keep walking. I'm hyperventilating. The streets are a blur.
	Then I bump into a man wearing a sheep-skin coat and a koppel. He has a bluetooth headset on.
	'Shit'… I think.
	'I've come to synagogue'…
	Maybe this is my time. I take a deep breath ready to be spiritually moved. I go to walk in.
SECURITY (L)	'Where do you think you are going?'
DAN	'To pray'
SECURITY (L)	'Pray?'
DAN	'Yeh.'
SECURITY (L)	'To who?'
DAN	'Woody Allen? Who do you think?'
SECURITY (L)	'Don't get funny with me. You're Jewish?'

DAN	'Why would I fake that?'
SECURITY (L)	'What was the most recent Jewish holiday?'
DAN	'Well my parents just got back from Marbella.'
SECURITY (L)	'That's it. Not coming in.'
DAN	'What? Come on. You wanna check?' (*Pointing at penis*.)
SECURITY (L)	'Not coming in.'
DAN	'I'm in mourning. My grandad just died. You don't know what I've just been through.'
SECURITY (L)	'Wish you long life. But you are not coming in… Can never be too careful nowadays.'
DAN	'Fine.' But as I walk away I notice an open window. I think I have schlapped this far. I peek in and see a young girl stood at the front in a colourful tallis with a Torah in front of her. She is singing… completely out of tune. I can't move away. I see her parents kvelling with pride, ready to explode. She sings and sings. The everlasting light shining above her head. She gets to the end. Says the blessing and sweets are thrown at her. One ricochets off the bald patch of the doting father and flies out the window. As I suck on the boiled sweet. The girl… now, woman says:

BAT MITZVAH GIRL (L) 'I will now translate.'

DAN Her voice cracking, tongue getting caught on the elastic band linked to her braces...

BAT MITZVAH GIRL (L) '*Devarim*, Chapter 32, Verses 36 to 39:
"For Adonoy will vindicate God's people
And take revenge for God's servants,
Upon seeing that their might is gone,
And neither bond nor free is left.
[God] will say: Where are their gods,
The rock in whom they sought refuge,
Who ate the fat of their offerings
And drank their libation wine?
Let them rise up to your help,
And let them be a shield unto you!

See, then, that I, I am the One;
There is no god beside Me.
I deal death and give life;
I wounded and I will heal:
None can deliver from My hand."'

DAN The man with the bluetooth headset has spotted me on his patrol round.

SECURITY (L) 'Oi, what do you think you're doing? Piss off.'

DAN 'But...' I jump down and head towards home.

SECURITY (L) 'And don't you ever ever come back.'

LAUREN I peel myself off the floor. I'm desperate for a shower.

But the boiler. Still broken.

I should have let him fix it first. I go to West Hampstead. Joshua's house.

JOSHUA (D) 'Come to give back your winnings?'

REVENGE: AFTER THE LEVOYAH

LAUREN	'I've come for a shower.'
JOSHUA (D)	'Oh, Lauren. Of course.'
LAUREN	'Thanks.'
JOSHUA (D)	'My pleasure.'
LAUREN	I get into the shower. Green tiles. I turn on the brass taps and use his Jo Malone shower gel. I feel like in this moment I should be trying to scrub what happened off me. But actually all I can think is… 'I'd do it again.'
	I get out of the shower and wrap the fluffy White Company towel around me. I step out of the bathroom.
	Joshua is stood there waiting for me.
JOSHUA (D)	'Hot chocolate?'
LAUREN	'Sure? Why not.'
	I notice he's got changed.
	Put on a shirt and some cologne.
JOSHUA (D)	'Listen, Lauren. I want to talk to you about something.'
LAUREN	(*To self.*) Oh god.
	'Sure.'
JOSHUA (D)	'Lauren, we have been friends a long time.'
LAUREN	'We have.'
JOSHUA (D)	'It's so funny you are here… I've been thinking about this.
	Thinking about how to say it.'
LAUREN	(*To audience.*) Oh god.

JOSHUA (D)	'We were each other's first kiss.'
LAUREN	'So?'
	He wasn't mine… he won a kiss in a game of poker.
	I've never lost to him since.
JOSHUA (D)	'Lauren, it has been set in stone since then.'
LAUREN	'You've lost it.'
JOSHUA (D)	'I know there is something between us.
	It's beshert. I've never been more sure of it.'
LAUREN	'What are you talking about, Josh?'
JOSHUA (D)	'I want you to marry me. Marry me, Lauren.'
LAUREN	'You are joking.'
JOSHUA (D)	'I want you to marry me. My parents have just bought two flats in Herzliya. One for them. One for us.
	Come with me.'
LAUREN	'You must be joking.'
JOSHUA (D)	'I am deadly serious. My parents have spoken to your parents.'
LAUREN	'They haven't.'
JOSHUA (D)	'They have. They're into it.'
LAUREN	'Then let them go with you.'
JOSHUA (D)	'Don't worry we will have a room for them. We'll need some extra hands when the babies arrive.'
	'Well, we could leave right away. BA sale is on.
	I could book us onto a flight now.'

LAUREN	I think about the dead plumber. His family. The police turning up. Asking if I've seen him. A search warrant. A speck of blood. Dan not being able to take the heat. Telling the police everything. Going down for murder. Life in prison.
	This could be my escape. I could get out of here. I think of flying to Tel Aviv. Getting a cab to Herzliya. A new life. A new start.
	Then I think of that place. Living there… with Joshua…
	'Nope, I'd rather stay here and take my chances.'
JOSHUA (D)	'What?'
LAUREN	'I am not coming with you.'
JOSHUA (D)	'Why not?'
LAUREN	'I don't need to give you a reason.'
JOSHUA (D)	'Well, it's a very generous offer.'
LAUREN	'So you say.'
JOSHUA (D)	'Look, I have made a spreadsheet of finances. A map of the area, look. We are right by a nursery. There are communal bomb shelters of course, we can play Scrabble down there.'
LAUREN	'Joshua. Stop.'
JOSHUA (D)	'Look, Lauren. This could be the best offer you get.'
LAUREN	'We'll see.'
JOSHUA (D)	'It's not safe here.'
LAUREN	'I agree. So I'm going.'
JOSHUA (D)	'I meant…'

LAUREN	'I know. Josh. I know what you meant. But look. I am here. In a towel and you are asking me to move away? Telling me we are going to be married. Suggesting I leave it all. Leave my home. Leave all I know. For what? A spreadsheet and a hot chocolate?'
JOSHUA (D)	'I want what's best for you. Soon there will be nothing for you here.

There is nothing for you here now.' |
| LAUREN | 'The quicker you get on that plane the better.' |
| JOSHUA (D) | 'This is the biggest mistake of your life.' |
| LAUREN | 'Let's hope so.'

I go to get dressed…

'Do you mind?' |
JOSHUA (D)	'Fine.'
LAUREN	I leave. I go home. I see Dan's shoes in the hall. I go to bed. In the morning I hand Dan his coat,'We are going.'
DAN	'Fine.'
LAUREN	Dan drives.

The address leads us to an industrial estate in Canning Town. Malcolm stood outside the warehouse. Having a fag. |
MALCOLM (D)	'Here they are, Ronnie and Reggie.'
LAUREN	He winks.
MALCOLM (D)	'Get in there, everyone is waiting.'
LAUREN	We make our way inside the warehouse.
DAN	It's cold. Colder than it was outside.

LAUREN	Boxes line the walls.
DAN	Catnip. Boxes of catnip.
LAUREN	In the middle of the room are a semi-circle of folding chairs with someone sat in each one.
	We are last to arrive. We sit in the only empty chairs.
DAN	Malcolm follows us. He stands in front of us all by a blackboard.
LAUREN	He coughs, looks around at us all.
MALCOLM (D)	'I have had enough. I have had it up to here. I'm an old man now.
	Do I need this level of stress any more? No. Enough is enough.
	It is time to take matters into our own lappers.
	You. You are all here for a reason. We are here to stop this madness. To put a cork in it. It is getting worse and worse and we need to put an end to it once and for all.
	For the job at hand. I have assembled a top group of yids.
	Each one of you is here for a reason.'
LAUREN	I look at the rest of the people there.
MALCOLM (D)	'My right-hand man Moishy.'
LAUREN	Moishy is sat with his feet barely touching the ground.
MOISHY (L)	'If you want to get to Malcolm, you have to go through me first.'
LAUREN	He's wearing a brown duffle coat and it seems like every pocket has a mobile

	phone in it. For a man in his nineties it's like every part of him is a muscle. Even his head.
MALCOLM (D)	'Next we have Sara.'
LAUREN	Sara is sat in a long dress and a thick brown bob of hair.
MALCOLM (D)	'She owns half of Stamford Hill.'
SARA (D)	'The nice half.'
LAUREN	Behind her are two giant chassids.
DAN	The tallest I've ever seen.
LAUREN	Each with a long black overcoat a black hat and thick beard.
DAN	The one on the right puts a fag in Sara's mouth.
LAUREN	The one on the left lights it.
MALCOLM (D)	'And let's just say she didn't get it by playing nicely. She's shrewd, cool and has a whole army of tough fucking frummers who will give their lives for her.'
SARA (D)	'Me and Malcolm go way back. I would do anything for him.
	Malcolm sorted my divorce when my ex-husband wouldn't give me a get.'
MALCOLM (D)	'How is Hershel anyway?'
SARA (D)	'Doctors say inconclusive.'
MALCOLM (D)	'Send him my love.'
	'Next is Simon.'
LAUREN	Simon is sat there in an immaculate suit, stomach popping out of his shirt , his head still raw from from what looks like hair transplant surgery.

SIMON (D)	'I flew straight in from Turkey to be here. I'm going back to get my teeth done next.'
LAUREN	He takes out his phone and using his index finger only types out and sends a message.
MALCOLM (D)	'Simon is a city boy. Swapped selling batteries on the Roman Road for stock broking. Fish and chips for Thatcher and Stepney for Chigwell.
	He can get anyone, and I mean anyone, on the other end of that phone.'
SIMON (D)	'I've put money behind Malcolm for years. When I heard this idea. How could I resist?'
MALCOLM	'Next to him is Rabbi Sonya.'
LAUREN	Now this is a woman with long brown hair, a colourful woven kippah and Dr. Martens on.
SONYA (L)	'Ey up.'
DAN	Sonya leads at one of the biggest liberal shuls in London.
LAUREN	She did our cousin Charlotte's Bat Mitzvah.
DAN	Plays fantastic guitar.
MALCOLM (D)	'In her youth she was a fighter for Antifa. Known for being able to make a Molotov cocktail out of a bottle of Palwins wine.'
SONYA (L)	'We used to call it a mazel tov cocktail.'
MALCOLM (D)	'Now she's got a shul we can use for our decoy event and knows how to handle herself if needs be.'
SONYA (L)	'For the record. I am not sure about the goal of this.

	I mean. I don't actually think he is that bad.'
MALCOLM (D)	'Eh?'
SONYA (L)	'Stupid maybe. Who doesn't want free broadband for god's sake.
	But my congregation… loathe him.
	And as a hopeful candidate to lead the liberal Jewish movement, I could certainly use the brownie points.
	Plus, Malcolm sorts my parking tickets around shul on a Saturday, traffic wardens nonstop.'
MALCOLM (D)	'This is Dan and Lauren, their grandfather just died. Gotta get them out the house. Dan's driving. And Lauren, Lauren is dangerous.
	And me…
	I am Malcolm Spivak.
	Here's the plan.'
LAUREN	He spins round the blackboards to show a blueprint and right in the middle is a photo of the Labour leader. Jeremy Corbyn. In black and white.
DAN	My heart sinks. It's actually happening.
LAUREN	I'm looking around the room as people are nodding, smiling and taking down notes.
DAN	Then I hear the words… 'kidnap… torture ransom.' Moishy laughs.
LAUREN	The room falls into a barrage of bickering and shouting, everyone with their own plan on what to do with him, why they are doing it and exactly how severe they

	should be. Malcolm stands at the front pointing at the board.
	I notice Dan has got his hand up. No one pays attention and he puts his hand up as high as it can go, like a kid in school who really needs the toilet.
	Then he starts going…'
DAN	'Excuse me… Excuse me… Excuse me…'
LAUREN	Unable to cope with the patheticness of it all, I put my hands around my mouth and shout:
	'Shut uuuuup!'
	The room falls silent.
DAN	'Thanks, are you sure about all of this?'
LAUREN	'Dan, shut it.'
MALCOLM (D)	'It is time. We have been fucked about too much now. And I am at the end of my tether. It's all over the news. People are terrified. Shitting themselves that this racist will be prime minister.'
DAN	'Is he though? Racist?'
LAUREN	'Shut up, Dan. Are you really going to question someone who has killed Nazis?
MALCOLM (D)	'Do you want to sit on your arse and do nothing? Be nothing.
	Or do you want to be one of the ones who is remembered. Who did something. Who stood up for what they believed in and did something about it? Ay… do you?
	I want you here. But if you don't want in. That's fine. Just fuck off and keep your mouth shut. And remember who helped you with that yok plumber.'

LAUREN	'Malcolm. We are in. Yes. One hundred per cent.'
DAN	'Lauren.'
LAUREN	'Dan.'
DAN	I look at the others.
LAUREN	These are people who want to do something, who have already done something, people who have had enough.
	I look at Dan. I want him to, I need him to…
	'Dan. Daniel. You're in.'
DAN	'Okay… okay… I'm in.'
	I sit back down.
LAUREN	'Thank god.'
MALCOLM (D)	'Shekoya. Let's get down to gesheft.'
DAN	It's two days later. Our alarms go off at six a.m.
LAUREN	'Dan, we need to go.'
DAN	I grab Popa's golf club. We go.
LAUREN	The day before Sonya sent Corbyn's office an invite to a fake Holocaust memorial event.
DAN	Simon used his contacts to get this invite to the top of the pile. It was put in Corbyn's diary right away.
LAUREN	Simon got every paper to call saying they'd be there.
DAN	What a photo opportunity.
LAUREN	If he'd turned it down it would have been more trouble than it's worth.

DAN	And of course, what would make this all the more tempting.
LAUREN	A real-life Holocaust survivor. Moishy.
DAN	I arrive to pick up Malcolm at eight a.m.
	He's waiting outside of the door dressed as a traffic warden.
	Glaring at his watch.
MALCOLM (D)	'Come on get in the van. Get a fucking move on. We don't have much time.'
LAUREN	Corbyn took the bait. And to show off his green credentials he agreed to pick up Moishy from his flat in Gants Hill.
DAN	Lauren is going to go to Moishy's and act as his granddaughter and minder.
LAUREN	While Dan is driving Malcolm.
DAN	Lauren heads over to Moishy's early doors and waits to be picked up by Corbyn's chauffeur in a Prius.
LAUREN	Corbyn arrives arrive bang on time.
	I text Malcolm
	'Jonah is in the whale.'
DAN	We are speeding towards the meeting point, Dagim's the Fishmonger's. In a side road nearby, Sara has stationed all her heavies in Volvo minivans ready to surround the Prius and obscure the abduction.
	Sara awaits Lauren's signal.
LAUREN	Just before we go down the side road I text Sara.
	'NOW.'

	And the road fills with the Volvos. We are totally surrounded.
	Moishy is really laying it on thick.
MOISHY (L)	'Vot is going on? Can't we get to the synagogue? Vot day is it?'
DAN	Me and Malcolm arrive at Dagim's just in time.
LAUREN	Once Moishy has checked there's no one around, he gives the signal. We put on our gas masks and Moishy releases a sleeping gas, knocks Corbyn and the driver out.
DAN	Malcolm dressed as the traffic warden opens the door of the Prius.
LAUREN	Me and Moishy drag Jeremy Corbyn into the van and we all drive away. Just like that.
DAN	I am shaking whilst driving.
MALCOLM (D)	'Ease up. Deep breaths.'
MOISHY (L)	'A treat it worked.'
DAN	As we hit the North Circular, a black Mercedes hits the side of the car.
MALCOLM (D)	'What the fuck was that?'
MOISHY (L)	'Eyes on the road. Look.'
DAN	It hits our car again.
	And again.
	I am trying to keep the steering wheel straight.
LAUREN	I try and see what is going on. Two angry people in black suits and sunglasses are in the front. Another in the back pops his head out the window holding a gun. They have a gun!

MALCOLM (D)	'Fuck 'em.'
DAN	'Shit. Shit.'
MALCOLM (D)	'FUCK OFF. Dan, put your foot down.'
DAN	'Shit. Shit.'
LAUREN	They speed up next to us and start bashing the side of the van.
DAN	I am desperately trying to keep the van straight.
LAUREN	The person in the back with the gun is attempting to take aim at Dan.
	'He's going to shoot!'
DAN	'Tell Mum she didn't need to put Fluffy down. It was me that stained the carpet all those years ago. I'm sorry'
MALCOLM (D)	'That's our turning. We need to lose the pricks.'
MOISHY (L)	'Enough already.'
LAUREN	Moishy rustles through his bag and takes out a jar of purple stuff… chrain.
MOISHY (L)	'I was saving this for lunch.'
DAN	Moishy holds the jar over his head and lobs it. It careens through the air heading towards the Merc.
LAUREN	It hits the windscreen of the car.
	As it does the jar smashes and the front of the car is covered in purple.
DAN	The car swerves.
LAUREN	Swerves again.
DAN	And again.

LAUREN	Until it spins once, twice, hits the hard shoulder.
DAN	And explodes.
MALCOLM (D)	'Say hello to Lenny for me, fuckers! Dan, concentrate.'
DAN	I'm hyperventilating.
MALCOLM (D)	'Well done, Moishy.'
MOISHY (L)	'I guess they were feeling a little horse… radish.'
DAN	We finally get off the motorway and park up the van by the industrial estate. I get out of the car and throw up immediately.
LAUREN	One of the frummers gives him a bottle of water.
DAN	'Thanks.'
LAUREN	We bundle our hostage into the building…
	We have him on a chair.
	Malcolm gives him a thump around the head.
DAN	Moishy gives him a pinch.
	Sonya kneels opposite him.
SONYA (L)	'Hello. Do you know why you are here?'
SIMON (D)	'Course he don't.'
LAUREN	Says Simon as he rolls up his sleeves to expose a tattoo of Margaret Thatcher wearing a Tottenham Hotspurs kit.
SONYA (L)	'We are very unhappy.'
MALCOLM (D)	'He's a cunt.'
SONYA (L)	'Please, calm down.'

MALCOLM (D)	'Sorry, Rabbi.'
SONYA (L)	'Listen we are very unhappy with the way you have been presenting yourself. The way you have been treating us.
	You think you can get away with it? You think you can get around it like that.'
LAUREN	Thump.
MALCOLM (D)	'Can't understand irony... Well isn't this ironic...'
LAUREN	Thump.
LAUREN	Malcolm pulls out a big metal rod.
MALCOLM (D)	'See this, I am gonna smash you in the head with it. Or I might do your kneecaps. Or I might shove it up your –'
DAN	'– What the fuck? Stop.'
LAUREN	'Dan, this is it.'
DAN	'But why are we doing this?'
LAUREN	'Don't you get it yet?'
MALCOLM (D)	'He's a cunt. He has to go.'
MOISHY (L)	'What he said.'
LAUREN	'See, Dan?'
DAN	'But why him? Rabbi? Shed some light. Please.'
SONYA (L)	'I always liked him.'
MALCOLM (D)	'He hates Israel. You heard what he says.'
DAN	'Is that antisemitic?'
SONYA (L)	'I did a sermon criticising Israel a few years ago. I got called antisemitic. Nearly lost my job.'

MALCOLM (D)	'Well, are you?'
SONYA (L)	'To be honest I just don't know any more.'
MALCOLM (D)	'An antisemitic rabbi. Do me a favour.'
SIMON (D)	'You see what he wants to do to businesses. He wants to give all our hard-earned cash away to people who can't be bothered to get up off the sofa. We'll all be skint.'
MOISHY (L)	'What? What has that got to do with antisemitism?'
SIMON (D)	'I'm a Jew. And I don't like it. The taxes, the immigrants, all of it. He'll take everything we worked so hard for.'
MALCOLM (D)	'He's mates with Hamas.'
DAN	'You believe that?'
MALCOLM (D)	'Maybe… I dunno. Fuck it. Alan Sugar says he's as bad as Hitler.'
MOISHY (L)	'Hitler? I don't think.'
MALCOLM (D)	Whatever. People are terrified. It's his fault. Isn't it?'
DAN	'Is it?'
LAUREN	Just then a black cab smashes though the wall honking its horn.
MALCOLM (D)	'Fuck, what the fuck?'
LAUREN	In the front of the cab is Clive the Cabby. And he looks furious. His face is bright red. He is frothing at the side of the mouth, trying to open the door which is blocked by a pile of catnip boxes.

CLIVE (L)	'Hand him fucking over.'
LAUREN	In the back of the cab are a group of shaven-headed men. Including Alf from the shiva who is being held up like a puppet. Scrawled on the side of the cab in red marker is: 'Romford Friends of Israel.'
MALCOLM (D)	'Piss off.'
CLIVE (L)	'Hand him over.'
MALCOLM (D)	'Go fuck yourself.'
CLIVE (L)	'Alf, Alf. Hold up the gun.'
MALCOLM (D)	'He can't even hold his own schmakiel when he takes a piss.'
CLIVE (L)	'Give us that antisemite.'
MALCOLM (D)	'No he's our antisemite.'
DAN	'Lauren, what is happening?'
LAUREN	'Shut up.'
NAOMI (D)	'Stop in the name of JFJ.'
LAUREN	Attached to the ceiling by a rope are four people wearing walking boots, cargo trousers and red T-shirts. They are holding banners with rainbows, hammer and sickles and stars of davids. One of them reads: 'Jews for Jeremy.' Another has an image of a person laid on a chaise longue with a notebook. The banner reads, 'Union of Psychotherapists: Muswell Hill Division.'
NAOMI (D)	'We have come to rescue Mr Corbyn. Jeremy, don't panic.'

CLIVE (L)	'Not these kapos.'
LAUREN	Shouts Clive as he steers Alf to point the gun at them.
NAOMI (D)	'Hand him to us.'
CLIVE (L)	'No, hand him to us.'
MALCOLM (D)	'He's going nowhere.'
LAUREN	The abseiling activists carefully manoeuvre themselves down the wall.
	They finally get to the bottom and take out some leaflets.
NAOMI (D)	'Just give him over. We've got some literature for you to read.
	We think you'll find it most enlightening.'
MALCOLM (D)	'Fuck off.'
LAUREN	Just then the door is kicked in.
DAN	Jeremy Corbyn's eyes nearly pop out of his skull.
	In come five people all in the best shape I have ever seen.
	The boss is short, muscley and holding an Uzi.
	She lifts up her sunglasses to reveal bright-green eyes.
	She speaks in a thick Israeli accent.
MOSSAD (L)	'What is taking you all so long?'
MALCOLM (D)	'Who the fuck are you?'
MOSSAD (L)	'Malcolm Spivak, we are here from the Israeli government.'

MALCOLM (D)	'It's the fucking Mossad. You're the fucking Mossad. Do me a favour.'
MOSSAD (L)	'We have done you many favours so far. Do you really think you would have got this far if it was not for us. But now you must go through with this. If we can show that you Jews, you pathetic weak European Jews killed this man, people will think he is actually a Jew hater and thus will connect our cause to every Jew.'
MALCOLM (D)	'Fucking hell. So you helped us?'
MOSSAD (L)	'Of course we did. Your plan was stupid.'
MALCOLM (D)	'Shut up.'
MOSSAD (L)	'No you shut up.'
MALCOLM (D)	'You shut up. Well we ain't gonna kill him. You'll have to do it.'
MOSSAD (L)	'And how do you think that would look? If we wanted to do it, we would have done it years ago. Put a bomb in his lamp or toilet or something. You have to do it. Or you will be in big trouble… we know things.'
MALCOLM (D)	'Fuck off.
MOSSAD (L)	'Don't tell us to fuck off.'
MALCOLM (D)	'I can tell you what I want. You work for me don't you? Fuck off. I've given you wankers enough cash over the years. Put my pounds in that little fucking blue box. Now you fuck off.'

MOSSAD (L)	'How did you get that money, Malcolm.'
MALCOLM (D)	'Don't you start… I ain't afraid of your little toy. I've seen bigger guns in my sock drawer.'
LAUREN	In walk five men all in blue suits.
MALCOLM (D)	'And who the fuck are you?'
MI5 (L)	'Well we can't tell you who we are… but let's say our boss wears a crown.'
MALCOLM (D)	'Fuck me, it's MI5.'
MI5 (L)	'We did not say that.'
MALCOLM (D)	'Look at you, it's the yok patrol… what else. How did you know about this.'
MI5 (L)	'Well we had some help.'
MALCOLM (D)	'Who? Who's the fucking grass?'
SONYA (L)	'I'm sorry, Malcolm.'
MALCOLM (D)	'Not you, Rabbi.'
SONYA (L)	'They just had so much on me, Malcolm. And who knows, one day I might want to be in the Board of Deputies… or even a Labour MP. I had to cooperate.'
MALCOLM (D)	'If you weren't a rabbi, I'd skin you alive.'
MI5 (L)	'We have been wanting this man gone for a long time. He wouldn't even stand for the national anthem. We had to get rid of him somehow. We have been building a very structured English society… we couldn't have one man bring it all down. But we were lucky, this fool did some really stupid things.

	All we needed to do was make sure it was reported on… all the time… every day.
	Now you have to go through with it.'
MALCOLM (D)	'Well we're not going to… You do it.'
MI5 (L)	'Oh no, we don't do that sort of thing any more, just look at what happened with Princess Diana. Disaster.'
DAN	The Mossad agent shouts,
MOSSAD (L)	'Come on, yalla get on with it. Kill him.'
DAN	'Lauren, I think we should go now…'
LAUREN	'Not yet.'
DAN	From outside there is a huge noise. 'Is that a helicopter?'
LAUREN	In comes a man in a blue suit and aviator sunglasses.
CIA (D)	'Well, looks like the shit has really hit the fan.'
LAUREN	The Mossad agent and MI5 look embarrassed.
CIA (D)	'What have I told you two? You have to nip these things in the bud before they get out of hand. Have you learned nothing from Iraq and Afghanistan?'
MOSSAD (L)	'I know. We just want him gone.'
MI5 (L)	'Yes. We all do. But we can't do it.'
CIA (D)	'Of course you can't. Taking out a beloved socialist candidate from the inside is a very delicate operation.'

MALCOLM (D)	'Fucking hell. It's the CIA. Piss off, you stupid Yank.
	Ain't you got a hot-dog-eating competition to get to?
CIA (D)	'Malcolm Spivak. If I were you I wouldn't raise your voice with me.'
MI5 (L)	'Gosh, they're a bit crass.'
CIA (D)	'Resilient little critters aren't they.'
MI5 (L)	'They certainly do have their uses though.'
CIA (D)	'I had hoped they'd all be in the Holy Land by now. The End Times are a'comin.'
MALCOLM (D)	'Shut the fuck up. Do you know who I am?'
MI5 (L)	'We know exactly who you are.'
MALCOLM (D)	'Then you should know. No one tells Malcolm Spivak what to do.'
MI5 (L)	'Well, we have so far… why do you think you're here?'
MALCOLM (D)	'Shit…'
LAUREN	I look at the man cowering in his chair.
	I think about Popa Lenny. I think about Nana, not wanting to leave the flat. Joshua, my parents.
	I think about Dartford.
	I think about everyone before me who has taken action. Everyone who has fought for something better.
	It feels like a chain of hands as I take the golf club.

DAN	'What are you doing?'
LAUREN	I say:
	'A time comes in every yid's life where they either sit around and do fuck all and wait for something awful to happen, or they do something. Stand up and fucking do something.'
DAN	'What? What are you talking about? Lauren? No. Not like this…'
LAUREN	I raise the golf club over my head… it is shaking in the air.
DAN	'Lauren. No. Stop'
LAUREN	I can feel the club about to come down. All my weight is behind it.
DAN	'That poor man.'
LAUREN	I feel all eyes on me as the club is now inches from his head.
DAN	I can't let my sister do this.
LAUREN	Just as I am about to make impact. I feel a jolt on my arm.
DAN	I push her away from hitting him. Push her arm.
LAUREN	I go flying. Club first. I trip over my feet, lose all control.
DAN	Lauren is moving around like she is pissed, club in hand.
	She falls straight into the Mossad agent.
LAUREN	The golf club hits the Uzi which gives off shots.
DAN	The Mossad agent gives a shriek.

LAUREN	It's like time has slowed down as the bullets leave the gun.
DAN	'Fuck.'
LAUREN	I get back to my feet.
DAN	The bullets are streaming through the air.
LAUREN	The bullets fly past me, past Dan. And are heading straight towards Malcolm.
MALCOLM (D)	'Moishy, Moishy, get out the fucking way.'
MOISHY (L)	'Ergh. You got me. Oh I am hit. I am hit.'
MALCOLM (D)	'He's a fucking survivor, you cunt. Moishy, Moishy, talk to me. Talk to me.'
MOISHY (L)	'This is the end, Malcolm. Malcolm. The end for me. It has been wonderful knowing you. All the good times. All the business.'
MALCOLM (D)	'No, Moishy. No. You are too young. You got too much life in you yet.'
MOISHY (L)	'End this for me, Malcolm.'
DAN	All the life exits from Moishy's body and he goes completely limp.
LAUREN	Malcolm gives the lifeless corpse one last hug and gently places him on the ground. He slowly gets up and says,
MALCOLM (D)	'Rabbi… please.'
SONYA (L)	'Of course.'
	RABBI SONYA *recites the Kaddish quietly during* MALCOLM*'s speech.*
	They don't need to line up perfectly but the final 'amien'/'amen' should be in unison.

MALCOLM	SONYA
Kids, you two get out of here.	*Yitgaddal v'yitkaddash sh'meih rabba (amen).*
It's about to get ugly.	
For years and years I have been told what to do. What to think.	*b'alma di v'ra chiruteih, v'yamlich malchuteih, b'chayyeichon uv 'yomeichon uv'chayyei di chol beit yisra'el, ba'agala u'vizman kariv, v'imru: amen.*
If it wasn't the rabbis, it was frummers. If it wasn't them, the police. If not them, you mob telling me what kind of person I could be. What kind of Yid I could be. Who I could know. Who I need to be afraid of.	*Y'hei sh'meih rabba m'varach, l'alam ul'almei almaya.*
	Yitbarach v'yishtabbach v'yitpa'ar v'yitromam v'yitnassei v'yit-haddar v'yit'alleh v'yit-hallal, sh'meih di kudsha, b'rich hu,
My name is Malcolm Spivak. Know what Spivak means? Singer, Cantor.	
I come from a line of men who would stand in the shul and sing and be listened to. People would look on in awe at their singing.	*l'eilla min kol birchata v'shirata, tushb'chata v'nechemata, di amiran b'alma, v'imru: amen.*
Now it is time. It is time for me to take on my family name.	*Y'hei sh'lama rabba min sh'maya, v'chayyim aleinu v'al kol yisra'el, v'imru: amen.*
It is time for you all to listen to me.	
Cos I am fucked off.	*Oseh shalom bimromav, hu ya'aseh shalom aleinu v'al kol yisra'el, v'al kol ha-olam, v'imru:*
Amien.	*Amen.*

LAUREN	Just then he opens up his jacket to reveal that strapped to his body are two machine guns, three revolvers, a machete, a bunch of grenades and a bazooka.

DAN	'I thought he was walking slowly.'
LAUREN	'Yeh, I thought it was the illness.'
MALCOLM (D)	'Lauren, Dan. Get the fuck out of here.'
LAUREN	'Okay, now it's time to go home.'
MALCOLM (D)	'Sonya, Sara. Simon. Catch.'
DAN	He throws them each a gun.
LAUREN	Everyone in the room is now pointing a gun at someone else.
	'Dan. Let's go.'
DAN	'What about him?'
LAUREN	'Who?'
DAN	'Him…'
	Pointing at Jeremy Corbyn.
LAUREN	'What about him?'
DAN	'We can't just leave him here… tied up, can we?'
LAUREN	'Why not?'
DAN	'Lauren.'
LAUREN	'Fine.'
DAN	We grab the tied-up politician and drag him to the door.
	Just as we reach it, we heard the first bang.
LAUREN	We hear a chorus of gunshots, explosions and screams.
DAN	'He said he wanted to go out with a bang.'
LAUREN	'I'm missing all the action.'
DAN	'Please go back if you want.'
LAUREN	'What we gonna do with this schmok?'

DAN	'I dunno. I couldn't leave him there.'
LAUREN	'Dan, he's an antisemite.'
DAN	'Is he?'
LAUREN	'I dunno.'
DAN	'Me either.'
DAN	A light is shining on us from above, along with a deafening sound that is getting closer and closer.
LAUREN	'Look.'
DAN	Above us is a green camouflage helicopter with an American flag painted on the back.
LAUREN	A ladder is thrown down from it.
DAN	When our eyes have adjusted to the light, we see piloting the helicopter…
	'Is that Moishy? …and where did he get that cigar?'
	The three of us climb the ladder.
LAUREN	Another explosion goes off behind us.
	Malcolm is sent flying. He hits the floor with a big thud.
	He slowly lifts his head. Both eyes black, missing teeth and blood all over his face.
MALCOLM (D)	'Moishy, I fucking knew it.'
MOISHY (L)	'Pleasure working with you Malcolm.'
MALCOLM (D)	'Godspeed boychik. Here, give us that cigar.'
LAUREN	Moishy throws the cigar out of the chopper.
	It's like it's floating in the air.
	Malcolm catches it with his teeth.

MALCOLM (D)	'Now the lot of you. Get the fuck out of here.'
MOISHY (L)	'I've been waiting for something like that for years. I faked dying and left my dentures.
	At least now I'll have the police off my back.'
DAN	'Fucking hell, Moishy. What just happened.'
LAUREN	'Are we going to be okay?'
MOISHY (L)	'Who knows.'
DAN	'"Who knows?" What do you mean "who knows?" That's it? Who knows… the Mossad… MI5… CIA. Who knows. What happened?
	Am I going to get arrested? I don't wanna go to prison.
	Oh my god, I think my nose is bleeding.'
LAUREN	'Calm down, Dan'.
DAN	'Calm down. Don't tell me to calm down.'
MOISHY (L)	'Will you shut your mouth? I am trying to drive this thing.'
DAN	'Sorry… Sorry…
	Moishy, Moishy? Wanna say something wise?
	Something that sums this all up?'
LAUREN	'Yeh, something like, "We Jews have to reckon with our intergenerational trauma or else we will be doomed to repeat the same cycles of violence forever"?'

MOISHY (L)	'How should I know? Listen. I am ninety-four still running. Running away trying not to get caught.
	Flying a fucking helicopter for the first time in my life. All I want is to go and have a nice tuna sandwich. Do you think we could have some nice peace and quiet for a bit?
	My song's about to come on.'
	MOISHY *turns on the radio. 'You Always Hurt the One You Love' sung by Des O'Connor comes on through the static.*
DAN	The four of us sit in silence in the helicopter as we fly over London.
LAUREN	With the sound of explosions, gunshots, sirens, and Des O'Connor.
DAN	And I think to myself, 'At least things can't get any worse.'

A Nick Hern Book

REVENGE: After the Levoyah first published in Great Britain in 2025 as a paperback original by Nick Hern Books Limited, The Glasshouse, 49a Goldhawk Road, London W12 8QP

REVENGE: After the Levoyah copyright © 2025 Nick Cassenbaum

Nick Cassenbaum has asserted his moral right to be identified as the author of this work

Cover photography by Christa Holka. Design by Laura Whitehouse mightyfinedesign.org

Designed and typeset by Nick Hern Books, London
Printed in the UK by Mimeo Ltd, Huntingdon, Cambridgeshire PE29 6XX

A CIP catalogue record for this book is available from the British Library

ISBN 978 1 83904 430 4

CAUTION All rights whatsoever in this play are strictly reserved. Requests to reproduce the text in whole or in part should be addressed to the publisher.

Amateur Performing Rights Applications for performance, including readings and excerpts, by amateurs in the English language throughout the world should be addressed to the Performing Rights Department, Nick Hern Books, The Glasshouse, 49a Goldhawk Road, London W12 8QP, *tel* +44 (0)20 8749 4953, *email* rights@nickhernbooks.co.uk, except as follows:

Australia: ORiGiN Theatrical, Level 1, 213 Clarence Street, Sydney NSW 2000, *tel* +61 (2) 8514 5201, *email* enquiries@originmusic.com.au, *web* www.origintheatrical.com.au

New Zealand: Play Bureau, 20 Rua Street, Mangapapa, Gisborne, 4010, *tel* +64 21 258 3998, *email* info@playbureau.com

United States and Canada: Howard Gooding at Blue Posts Management, see details below

Professional Performing Rights Applications for performance by professionals in any medium and in any language throughout the world (and by amateurs in the United States of America and Canada) should be addressed to Blue Posts Management Limited, 98 Hanover Road, London NW10 3DP, www.bluepostsmanagement.com

No performance of any kind may be given unless a licence has been obtained. Applications should be made before rehearsals begin. Publication of this play does not necessarily indicate its availability for amateur performance.

www.nickhernbooks.co.uk/environmental-policy